C000176282

World famous not just as a military academy but as the training ground of future statesmen and rulers – Winston Churchill trained here, as did King Hussein and his son the current King Abdullah II of Jordan – the Royal Military Academy Sandhurst is a national icon; its imposing Grand Entrance instantly recognisable around the world. It can trace its antecedents back more than 270 years and its presence in its current location more than 200.

Today it continues to train and educate officers for the British Army. Indeed, all those commissioned into the British Army, whether regular or reserve, direct entry from school or university, or commissioned from the ranks, and including those with specialist professional qualifications such as doctors, lawyers and chaplains, today pass through Sandhurst. It is truly the home of the British Army's officer corps. It is further enriched by the presence on its commissioning course of those from overseas – around 25 officer cadets in each intake, from 15–20 countries. Its preparation of today's young men and women for the rigours of junior leadership in contemporary conflict is professional and modern, but it takes pride in its history and draws inspiration from its past.

Front cover: Old College.
Left: The Sovereign's Parade at which the Senior Term receive their commissions.

THE SHOP: THE ROYAL MILITARY ACADEMY AT WOOLWICH

The formal training and education of British Army officers can be traced back to 1741 when, on the orders of King George II (the last reigning British monarch to serve on the field of battle – at Dettingen in 1743), an institution was established at Woolwich, under control of the Board of Ordnance, to train Gentlemen Cadets destined to officer the Royal Artillery. In 1761 they were joined by those who would serve in the Corps of Royal Engineers. Formally entitled 'The Royal Military Academy' from 1764, Woolwich was better known by its nickname 'The Shop'. Formal officer training for these technical arms (and from 1920 the Royal Corps of Signals, too) continued until the outbreak of the Second World War in 1939.

Above: Contemporary engraving of The Shop – the 'Old' RMA, Woolwich, *c.*1741.
Below: The Royal Military College, Woolwich.

THE ROYAL MILITARY COLLEGE

Shocked at the poor understanding of their profession demonstrated by infantry and cavalry officers in the wars against revolutionary France at the end of the 18th century, Colonel John Gaspard Le Marchant (a Channel Islander) drew up plans for progressive education. A 'staff school' was the first element to be realised, opening at an inn in High Wycombe in 1799; this was to become the 'Senior Department' of the Royal Military College in 1801, and was quickly joined the following year by a 'Junior Department' at Great Marlow, training Gentlemen Cadets who could start their training aged between 13 and 15.

Right: Major General John Gaspard Le Marchant, Sandhurst's founding father.
Below: The Junior Department on parade at Marlow.

THE SITE AT SANDHURST

In 1801 William Pitt the Younger – in a deal that today might raise the eyebrows of the Public Accounts Committee – sold to the government for £8,460 an unproductive estate of land which he had himself purchased from impoverished relatives for just £2,600. This estate near the village of Sandhurst was to form the basis of the site we see today, and by 1812 the building now known as Old College had been completed and the 400 cadets of the Junior Department moved from Great Marlow.

Cadets at the Royal Military College, c.1812.

Le Marchant, by then a Major General, had been appointed the first Lieutenant Governor, but in 1811 he returned to operational service in the Peninsular War. He was killed leading a cavalry charge at Salamanca in 1812 – the year his dream came to fruition with the opening of the Royal Military College at Sandhurst.

LATER DEVELOPMENTS

Le Marchant's Senior Department was to move to Sandhurst in 1821 where it remained part of the Royal Military College until 1862, when the Staff College opened as a separate establishment with its own building close to the estate's gate on the London Road (today the A30 through Camberley). The Staff College remained there until amalgamation in 1997 with the Royal Air Force Staff College (Bracknell) and Royal Naval Staff College (Greenwich) into the Joint Services Command and Staff College (now part of the Defence Academy of the UK at Shrivenham).

The Royal Military College continued to train officers for the Infantry and Cavalry (including, from 1862, those for the Indian Army) until its closure at the outbreak of the Second World War in 1939. Through the war years Sandhurst was home to two Officer Cadet Training Units (OCTUs).

Post-war, amalgamation of the Royal Military Academy Woolwich with the Royal Military College saw the opening on 3 January 1947 of the Royal Military Academy Sandhurst – with its now iconic motto 'Serve to Lead'. Its students were now styled 'officer cadets'.

Short Service Commission and National Service officers were trained at two Officer Cadet Schools: Mons (Aldershot) and Eaton Hall (near Chester). These combined at Mons in 1960, which was itself closed in 1972 with training concentrating at Sandhurst. In 1981 responsibility

for the officer training element of the Women's Royal Army Corps College (Bagshot) was transferred to the Commandant of Sandhurst and in 1984 the women's courses were physically moved to Sandhurst, too. With the introduction of a course at Sandhurst for Late Entry Officers (those commissioned from senior non-commissioned rank), Sandhurst truly became the home of the British Army's officer corps with all officers, regular and reserve, passing through it.

Above: Old College in the late 1800s.
Right: The York Town Gate from the London Road (now the A30).
Below: Old College today.

Easily the most identifiable building at Sandhurst, Old College was completed in 1812 to a design by William Wyatt, who also designed the 'new' Royal Military Academy buildings at Woolwich. The final design was executed by John Saunders, architect to the Barracks Department of the War Office. The frontage, in neo-classical style, is dominated by the portico leading to the Grand Entrance. The central building is flanked on either side by colonnades leading to smaller buildings and then on to pavilions. That at the western end (to your left as you look at Old College) was built as the official residence of the Lieutenant Governor and is today named Le Marchant House in honour of its first intended occupant. Sadly, General Le Marchant was killed before he could take up residence. That on the eastern end served as the infirmary and is today the Headquarters of Old College.

Behind the grand façade on either side, a series of corridors link to two 'tridents' housing the cadet accommodation. These, like the front buildings, consist of a basement and two stories. Beyond the Grand Entrance lies a double-height room that was once the College's chapel and is now the Indian Army Memorial Room.

Right: The Queen Victoria Statue with Old College beyond.
Below: One of the four bronze reliefs around the base of the Queen Victoria Statue: Royal Engineers blowing the Kashmir Gate in the Siege of Delhi (Indian Mutiny).

VICTORIA

1819-1901

QUEEN VICTORIA STATUE AND THE KING'S WALK

The statue of Queen Victoria in front of Old College at the bottom of the King's Walk was sculpted by Henry Price and unveiled in 1902, a year after the Queen's death, at the RMA Woolwich. It was moved to its present site in 1947. The bronze reliefs around the plinth depict batteries of Royal Horse Artillery in action in the South African and Second Afghan Wars, a mortar at the siege of Sebastopol during the Crimean War, and Royal Engineers blowing up the Kashmir Gate during the storming of Delhi in the Indian Mutiny.

An often repeated story – possibly apocryphal – has it that an overseas cadet (in some accounts the future King Hussein of Jordan) was reprimanded by his Platoon Colour Sergeant during drill for being 'idle on parade' and sent at the double to apologise to Queen Victoria. When he was later found asleep on his bed and asked, somewhat brusquely, what he thought he was doing, he responded that Her Majesty had told him he was looking rather tired and should rest for the remainder of the day!

The King's Walk leads from the Queen Victoria Statue to the south side of Old College parade square and is the formal approach for the sovereign or her representative at the Sovereign's Parade. It was given its current name after a visit by King George V, who chose to stop his car where the Queen Victoria Statue now stands and continue his journey on foot.

THE CANNONS

Along the front of the main building to either side of the portico, the parade square is overlooked by six Napoleonic-era cannons; the four closest to the entrance are British, while those at the extreme of either flank are French, both of which were captured at Waterloo.

Right: One of the French guns captured at the Battle of Waterloo.

Above: HRH the Countess of Wessex arrives at the Sovereign's Parade as the Queen's Representative.

THE PORTICO AND PEDIMENT

Surmounting the portico is a pediment decorated with the Royal cypher of King George III flanked by carvings of Mars and Minerva, the Roman god of war and goddess of wisdom. The steps leading up to the portico are perhaps most famous for the part they play in the Sovereign's Parade – the parade at which officer cadets receive their commissions at the completion of their training. At the conclusion of the parade the graduating cadets march in slow time up the steps and into the building. Since 1926 they have traditionally been followed by the Academy Adjutant – still mounted on his charger.

Right: The postbox, with Victorian cypher – built into the steps to the Grand Entrance – is still in use today.
Below: Mars and Minerva with the Royal cypher of George III between them.

THE GRAND ENTRANCE

Beyond the portico, through black gloss-painted double doors with polished brass fittings, one enters the Grand Entrance, lit by a central lantern and offering access to the west and east corridors, and, straight ahead as one enters, the Indian Army Memorial Room. Two pictures of particular note are hung here: to the left is Andrew Festing's portrait of Her Majesty the Queen, commissioned in 1991 (and unveiled the following year) to mark 250 years since the beginning of formal officer training at the RMA Woolwich; and on the right is Sergei Pavlenko's 'Royal Family Group'. Three generations of the Royal Family are shown gathered on the steps after Prince Harry's commissioning parade in 2006. The two trumpeters of the Household Cavalry in their state livery were reputedly added to the painting at the request of Her Majesty the Queen, who thought they would better frame the group.

Above: Inside the Grand Entrance.
Below: Sergei Pavlenko's 'Royal Family Group' on the occasion of Prince Harry's commissioning.

THE INDIAN ARMY MEMORIAL ROOM

Across the Grand Entrance, straight ahead as one enters, is the Indian Army Memorial Room. As perhaps the stained-glass windows suggest, this grand room was once the chapel of the Royal Military College, consecrated in 1813. By 1875 the number of cadets and staff had grown to such an extent that the chapel was no longer large enough to accommodate them and it was replaced in this function by a new chapel to the north – now incorporated into today's Royal Memorial Chapel – which was consecrated in 1879. The old chapel became a dining hall and would have been serving that role when Winston Churchill was a cadet here in the 1890s. It later became the Old College Library.

In 1948 it became a museum of the Indian Army and today is formally a memorial commemorating the legacy and service of the Gurkha and Indian regiments of the British Indian Army. It also now houses the very extensive collection of regimental insignia of the Indian Army, gathered over a 70-year period by Field Marshal Sir John Chapple and donated by the Field Marshal to the National Army Museum in 2013.

With its evocative paintings, crests and stained glass, and lit by a central chandelier and candelabra alternated with silver centre pieces, the Indian Army Memorial Room is a spectacular and memorable location for formal dinners.

Below: The Indian Army Memorial Room, originally the Royal Military College's Chapel.

The culmination of the Sovereign's Parade: following those who are being commissioned, the Adjutant, mounted on his charger, rides up the steps of Old College.

The central chandelier – made in 1957 from parts of older chandeliers – was presented as a gift from Peninsular and Oriental (P&O) and the British India Steam Navigation companies to commemorate those companies' long association with the British and Indian armies.

THE 'PRESTIGE ROOMS'

In the wings to either side of the Grand Entrance is a series of rooms, serving various functions, known collectively as the 'Prestige Rooms'. To the west, the Lord Room is a small conference/dining room named in memory of WO1 (Academy Sergeant Major) J.C. Lord, who served in the role of Academy Sergeant Major – the senior non-commissioned appointment in the British Army – from the Academy's formation in 1947 until 1963. Beyond this, the Overseas Room commemorates the many officer cadets from overseas who have graduated from Sandhurst before commissioning into their own countries' armies, many subsequently rising to senior rank. The room houses a collection of gifts to the Academy from visiting foreign Heads of State and senior military officers. Finally, in the west wing, the Marlborough Room, sometimes used as a company anteroom, celebrates John Churchill, 1st Duke of Marlborough

Above: Still mounted, the Academy Adjutant enters Old College.
Below: 'Waterloo' by Sir William Allan.

and one of Britain's greatest military heroes, whose finest victory, Blenheim, gives its name to one of the Academy's companies.

In the east wing, Sandhurst's founding father, Major General John Gaspard Le Marchant, is remembered in a room used as the Commandant's formal office in Old College. Beyond this and the History Room – a small museum of Sandhurst – is the Wellington Room. Like Marlborough's, the Iron Duke's greatest victory, Waterloo, is also a company name. Sir William Allan's famous painting of the 1815 battle from the British position hangs at one end of the room; at the other is a rather smaller print of Allan's picture of the battle from the French side – the original of that lives at Apsley House, the Duke of Wellington's London home.

OAK GROVE HOUSE AND LAKE HOUSE

Today, as a result of the planting and growth of trees and shrubs, and the removal of sections of the original sweeping connecting walls, Oak Grove House, off to the west of Old College, and Lake House, its mirror to the east, seem entirely separated from the main range and are joined only by architectural style. However, early prints show that the architectural vision was of one sweeping frontage.

Oak Grove House was built as a home for the Royal Military College's Paymaster, and Lake House for its Senior Medical Officer. At one time in the 1970s, Oak Grove House became noted as the first married home of HRH Princess Anne when she married Captain Mark Phillips, then an instructor at Sandhurst. Since the 1920s Lake House has traditionally been the home of the Academy Adjutant. Nearby, placed around an oak tree, are headstones in memory of the adjutants' chargers.

Left: Aerial view of the Academy today.
Below left: The Sandhurst History Room – a small but fascinating museum in Old College.
Below: Lake House, built for the Academy's Medical Officer but for many years now home to the Academy Adjutant.

NEW COLLEGE

If less iconic than its older neighbour, New College – built between 1908 and 1911 to a design by H.B. Measure, Director of Barack Construction – is nevertheless an imposing building. At its centre, surmounted by a domed clock tower, is the Academy Officers' Mess. The wings to either side were each built to house two companies. The military grandeur of the buildings – with echoes of Lutyen's New Delhi style – is enhanced by the presence on either side of the central entrance of 'tiger head' guns captured at Seringapatam in 1799.

The site chosen for the New College had once been used for the practice of entrenchments, so several miles of buried barbed wire had to be removed during construction. More than three million bricks were used, transported on a specially constructed railway branch from Blackwater station. The engine shed now forms part of the nearby Central Library. When New College was completed it was believed that it could boast the longest corridor in Europe.

From the opening of the Royal Military Academy Sandhurst in 1947 until 1970, what was then known as New Building housed both New College and Victory College. Victory College moved to the new 'East Building' in 1970. Shortly afterwards, Mons Officer Cadet School, responsible for Short Service and National Service officers, was closed and its functions moved to Sandhurst where for a brief period New College was known as 'Mons College'.

New College as seen from across the lake (left). The central block of New College now provides the Academy Officers' Mess.

THE LUNEBURG STONE

To the south side of the New College parade square, overlooking the extensive sports pitches, stands the Luneburg Stone. The plainness of this unprepossessing memorial belies its importance in world history since it originally marked the spot on Germany's Luneburg Heath where, on 5 May 1945, Field Marshal Montgomery received the formal surrender of all German forces in the Netherlands, north-west Germany and Denmark, effectively ending the Second World War in Europe. Montgomery had the memorial erected and then, in 1958, just before the British Army handed over control of the Luneburg Heath area to the West German government, he had it removed due to vandalism. It was brought to Sandhurst and unveiled in its current location in November 1958.

STATUE OF THE PRINCE IMPERIAL

The other notable memorial alongside New College parade square is the statue of Louis Napoleon, the Prince Imperial, son of the exiled Napoleon III of France. He had been a student at Woolwich and was killed in 1879 whilst attached as an observer to Lord Chelmsford's Headquarters in the Zulu War. Funded by subscription from officers and men from across the British Army, the statue was originally erected in Woolwich, being moved to its present site in 1955.

Right: Louis Napoleon, the Prince Imperial.
Below: The Luneburg Stone.

Unified by their brutalist concrete architectural style, to the south-east of New College stand Churchill Hall, the Victory Building (once Victory College and before that the 'East Building') and the Academy Headquarters.

Churchill Hall, the Academy's largest lecture theatre with a capacity of 1,200, was opened in 1970 by the Hon. Mrs Christopher Soames, Sir Winston Churchill's youngest daughter. In the opening address the Commandant of the day, Major General Phillip Tower, described Sir Winston as 'the most distinguished cadet that Sandhurst has yet produced'. So a central lecture theatre that plays so important a part in officer cadets' study here is a fitting and practical memorial. It has been the venue for lectures by Prime Ministers, visiting Heads of State and other prominent world figures. In 2013 Burmese opposition leader Aung San Suu Kyi addressed the Academy here.

Outside Churchill Hall sits the Academy's only tank – a Mark 6 Centurion of the sort in service with the British Army from 1945 until replaced by the Chieftain in the second half of the 1960s; variants remained in service with, for example, the Royal Engineers as late as the 1991 Gulf War. There are also two 5.5" Medium Guns, in service with the Royal Artillery from 1942 until 1981. Guns of this sort in service with 21 Army Group in 1944–45 fired more than 2.6 million shells between D-Day and the end of the war.

Victory Building, opened in 1970, was for some time called Victory College. With a capacity for four companies it was for many years home to commissioning courses for university graduates when they underwent separate courses from the non-graduates. Today there is no such segregation (with over 80 per cent of officer cadets being graduates) and Victory Building is home to a variety of short courses as well as providing overspill accommodation when needed. At one time its two large anterooms (each a social space for two companies of cadets) were named in honour of Captain Robert Nairac GC and Captain Richard Westmacott MC. Nairac and Westmacott were killed in Northern Ireland – Nairac abducted and murdered by the IRA while undertaking covert operations, and Westmacott killed during a shoot-out with an IRA gun team in Belfast while serving with the SAS. Today they are both remembered in the Northern Ireland Room, while the other anteroom has been converted into the South Atlantic lecture theatre, remembering those graduates of RMAS who died in the Falklands conflict.

It is ironic that the building least admired today for any aesthetic beauty is the only one at the Academy to have won an architectural award: Victory Building and the adjacent Academy

Churchill Hall: Sandhurst's main lecture theatre, named in memory of its greatest alumnus.

A Mark 6 Centurion stands guard over Churchill Hall.

MK 6 Centurion Tank

Technical Data

Headquarters were awarded Best Building of the Year by The Concrete Society in 1970.

The Academy Headquarters, adjacent to the Victory Building and of a complementary style, was designed by the same firm – Gollins, Melvin, Ward and Partners. Its façade is surmounted by a large-scale replica of the Academy cap-badge, with its motto 'Serve to Lead'. Inside, in pride of place on the main stairway, is hung a picture of Old College by David Napp, commissioned by the Sandhurst Foundation (now the Sandhurst Trust) to commemorate the Academy's bicentenary in 2012.

Left: David Napp's painting of Old College, commissioned by the Sandhurst Foundation (now the Sandhurst Trust) to commemorate Sandhurst's bicentenary.
Below: Academy Headquarters.

THE ROYAL MEMORIAL CHAPEL

When the Royal Military College's population outgrew its chapel – what is now the Indian Army Memorial Room – a new chapel was constructed in 1879 by the Royal Engineers, to a design inspired by a church in Florence. Unusually it was built with a south–north orientation, like the original chapel. When, after the Great War, it was enlarged, the alignment was changed closer to the traditional west–east layout, and what had been the chancel became, in effect, the crossing and transepts. The construction is of red brick with terracotta mouldings and the design, by Captain Arthur C. Martin, is Byzantine.

Although it was built as a memorial to the Gentlemen Cadets who had lost their lives in the First World War, it now stands as a memorial to all those who passed through the Academy and lost their lives in conflict. The names of 3,247 men commissioned at Sandhurst who died in the First World War are inscribed, by regiment and corps, on the pillars of the central chapel, while a roll of honour lists the 19,781 British and Commonwealth officers

The Royal Memorial Chapel.

THE LORD OF ALL LIFE,
CAME NOT TO BE SERVED BUT TO SERVE;
HELP US TO BE MASTERS OF OURSELVES
THAT WE MAY BE THE SERVANTS OF OTHERS,
AND TEACH US TO SERVE TO LEAD;
THROUGH THE SAME JESUS CHRIST, OUR LORD.
AMEN.

Above: The Academy Colours, lodged in the Chapel, beneath an inscription of the Collect – from which is drawn the motto 'Serve to Lead'.
Left: A service in the Royal Memorial Chapel.
Right: Inside the Royal Memorial Chapel.

who perished in the Second World War. Above the main doors – so as to be seen by all officer cadets as they leave the chapel – is the Collect of the Academy: 'Almighty God, whose son, the Lord of all life, came not to be served but to serve, help us to be masters of ourselves that we may be the servants of others, and teach us to serve to lead; through the same Jesus Christ, our Lord, Amen', from which is taken the Academy motto 'Serve to Lead'. On leaving the chapel, officer cadets come face-to-face with the memorial to those of non-commissioned rank who died in the two world wars – a poignant reminder of the duty and sacrifice of all ranks, of the responsibilities of command and of the bonds of loyalty between officers and those they are privileged to lead.

No visit to Sandhurst is complete without including the Royal Memorial Chapel – a majestic but sobering memorial to ultimate sacrifice, sometimes a centre of pomp and ceremony, but more often a place of quiet reflection.

THE ROMAN CATHOLIC CHAPEL OF CHRIST THE KING

Converted from a lecture room on the first floor of Old College, the Roman Catholic Chapel was opened in 1948 by the Cardinal Archbishop of Westminster, Cardinal Bernard Griffin. A major reworking of the interior and a new entrance stairway from Chapel Square were completed in 2004. The simplicity and dignity of the original chapel were retained in a fresh style which is at the same time contemporary and reverential. The dedication and blessing of the Foundation Stone occurred on 14 September 2004 in a service led by the Right Reverend Thomas Burns, Bishop of the Forces. His Serene Highness Prince Alois of Liechtenstein, an alumnus of the Academy who served with the Coldstream Guards, unveiled the stone.

Top: Entrance to the Roman Catholic Chapel of Christ the King.
Right: The Memorial to Other Ranks who lost their lives in the two world wars.

TO THE
GLORY OF GOD
AND IN
PROUD MEMORY
OF ALL
OTHER RANKS
WHO GAVE
THEIR LIVES
IN TWO
WORLD WARS
1914-18 · 1939-45

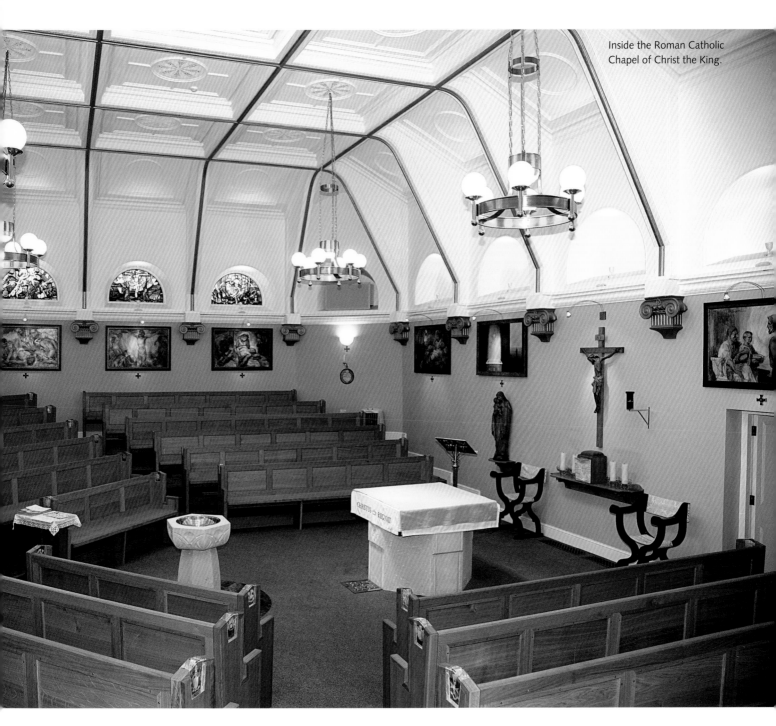

Inside the Roman Catholic Chapel of Christ the King.

GOVERNMENT HOUSE

Government House was built on the site of a considerably older farm complex, of which some of the original buildings – significantly altered over the years – still stand. Extensively renovated and remodelled in the years after the Royal Military College was opened, Government House became the official residence of the Governor, in place of Le Marchant House at the western end of Old College. The road from York Town to College Town, which had been public, was closed in order to connect Government House grounds to those of the College. Today it continues to serve as the residence of the Commandant.

Right: Government House, the official residence of the Commandant.
Below: The Medical Reception Station.

MEDICAL RECEPTION STATION

The Medical Reception Station is Sandhurst's own mini-hospital, providing primary and occupational health services for the staff and students of the Academy. Originally, an isolation hospital stood on this site, becoming the main hospital when that at the eastern side of Old College had to move to make way for more cadet accommodation in 1878. The current building was constructed in 1911 in the same red-brick and stone construction of nearby New College.

CENTRAL LIBRARY

Completed in 1863, the Central Library was actually built as the Royal Military College's gymnasium. It was converted to its present-day use in 1931 and has a collection of over 180,000 books, covering the history of (predominantly) land warfare, international affairs and contemporary conflict. To its rear, the Marlow Hall – named for the early home of the Junior Department – today forms an annex and reading room. However, it was originally the engine shed for the branch line that carried to site the building materials for New College.

The Central Library.

Inside the Former Army Staff College, and from outside (below).

FORMER ARMY STAFF COLLEGE (FASC)

Near to the Academy's main entrance on the A30 stands Sir James Penthorne's 1862 building which housed the Senior Division – later the Army Staff College. The Staff College moved out in 1997, amalgamating with the RN and RAF Staff Colleges to form the Joint Services Command and Staff College, now in a purpose-built flagship building at Shrivenham. Now known, somewhat prosaically, as the Former Army Staff College – or in Army acronym terms, FASC – today it houses the headquarters of the Army Medical Services, the Brigade of Gurkhas and other administrative departments. Close by, Staff College House, of similar vintage and architectural style, was built as the residence for the Staff College's Commandant.

Above: The Terrace today.
Left: The Terrace: Tea Caddy Row.

THE TERRACE

Running parallel to the modern A30 is a street of houses built to accommodate the senior staff of the Royal Military College. This attractive terrace of three-storey late Georgian houses soon attracted the nickname 'Tea Caddy Row', by which it is still commonly known. The entire row is Grade II listed and forms part of a conservation area.

As befits a place so replete with history and heritage, the extensive and beautiful grounds of Sandhurst are dotted with monuments and memorials. The more noteworthy of those not discussed elsewhere are highlighted here.

THE OVERSEAS CADET MEMORIAL

One of the more recent additions to the Academy grounds is the Overseas Cadet Memorial. Unveiled in June 2000 in the presence of the Jordanian Ambassador, it honours all those overseas officer cadets who have trained at Sandhurst. Designed by Michael Marriott FRBS, architecturally in plan it alludes to the four points of the compass to represent the very broad geographic spread of the countries whose officers have trained here, while in elevation the four concrete elements resemble shields representing strength and bravery. It is surmounted by gilded flame said to link the other elements and stand for integrity, strength and endurance. Today, roughly 25 overseas cadets are included in each intake from around 15–20 countries and overall more than 4,400 overseas cadets from more than 100 countries have been represented on courses here.

THE BOAR STATUE

In the Second World War XXX Corps' symbol was a charging black boar. The statue of a semi-reclining boar was 'liberated' from being a German garden ornament and used to mark the end of XXX Corps' main supply route

The Overseas Cadet Memorial.

Above: The XXX Corps Boar, and the Kurnool Mortar (right).

through the Netherlands and north-west Germany to Bremen (Route CLUB). It has sometimes been said that its relaxed posture – as opposed to the Corps official badge – was seen as especially apt, marking 'job done'! It was brought to Sandhurst in 1958 when XXX Corps, then part of the British Army of the Rhine, was disbanded, and has sat in its current location, at a fork in the main entrance road, since December 2000.

THE KURNOOL MORTAR

Weighing more than 8 tons and with a calibre of 27 inches, the Kurnool Mortar was captured by a British/Indian force in a minor conflict between the British Raj and the Nawab of Kurnool in 1839. Artillery aficionados argue that technically it is not a mortar at all but a howitzer, since its trunions (pivots) are at the mid-point not the base.

Around the Academy, places, people and former activities are remembered in the names of roads, buildings or areas. Principal among them are those listed below.

SLIM MESS

Secluded in the woodland beyond New College and Churchill Hall, the Slim Mess provides single living accommodation for the Academy's officers. It is named after Field Marshal 'Bill' Slim, most remembered for his inspirational leadership in commanding the 14th Army in Burma during the Second World War. His memoir *Defeat into Victory* is regarded as a seminal work on military leadership. Inside, the building is divided into four blocks: Soviet, Band, Isolation and Mortuary. They remember that in this area once stood buildings that housed the Soviet Studies Research Centre, the practice rooms for the RMAS resident band, the hospital's isolation ward and the mortuary.

FORT ROYAL

Fort Royal is today a modern building housing a café open to all and the junior ranks' restaurant, but the name recalls the fortification that once stood nearby – not, as is sometimes supposed, the now wooded mound diagonally opposite, but beyond that and beside the polo club stables – where defensive and siege warfare could be taught and practised.

WOOLWICH HALL

Next to the modern Fort Royal the Woolwich Hall memorialises one of RMAS's historic predecessors, the Royal Military Academy Woolwich, which trained officers for the Royal Artillery and Royal Engineers – once the only professionally trained officers in the Army – from 1741. Serving today as a lecture theatre, the somewhat nondescript building was once one of several indoor riding schools, recalling that equitation, still a sport keenly enjoyed at Sandhurst, was once a core part of the curriculum. The remaining indoor school and one of two stable complexes are across the road.

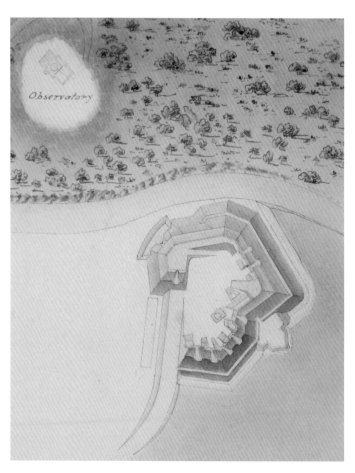

Sketch of Fort Royal, which once stood on the now wooded mound behind Old College. Also shown is David Narrien's Observatory.

The Montgomery Gymnasium.

SCOVELL LINES

Close to the Academy's College Town gate, Scovell Lines is the working accommodation of 44 Squadron, Royal Logistic Corps, providing transport support to the Academy. The name remembers General Sir George Scovell. As a junior officer on Wellington's staff in the Peninsular War, Scovell was largely responsible for cracking the codes used in the French army's correspondence with Paris, giving Wellington a significant intelligence advantage. In later life he was the Lieutenant-Governor then Governor of the Royal Military College and he is buried in the Academy cemetery.

FARADAY HALL

The bland, utilitarian building behind New College, housing Sandhurst's Academic Departments – War Studies, Defence and International Affairs, and Communications and Applied Behavioural Science – has all the charm of a 1960s polytechnic but is named for one of Britain's greatest scientists, Michael Faraday, who was Professor of Chemistry at the Royal Military Academy Woolwich from 1830–51. While perhaps not destined for quite such celebrity, today's academic staff are all experts in their fields and many of their predecessors – such as John Keegan and Richard Holmes – have gone on to be publicly as well as academically acclaimed authors and broadcasters.

MONTGOMERY GYMNASIUM AND MONS HALL

The Academy's main gymnasium facility is named in memory of Field Marshal Viscount Montgomery of Alamein, while the nearby annex Mons Hall commemorates Mons Officer Cadet School, which trained Short Service and National Service officers

Above: The Qaboos Pavilion, named for Sultan Qaboos of Oman.
Right: Engineer's sketch of Fort Narrien, one of several full-size mock-ups of fortifications in which cadets learned about defensive works and siege-craft.

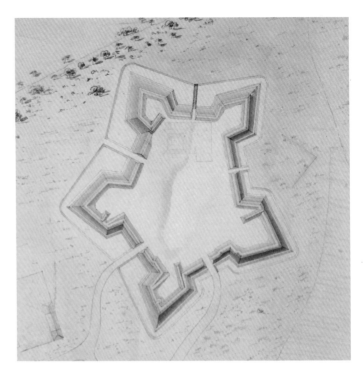

until it was amalgamated into Sandhurst in 1972. Part of Mons Hall is now named the King Hamad Hall in recognition of a donation from His Majesty King Hamad of Bahrain for its renovation and re-equipping. His Majesty – who is also Patron of the Sandhurst Trust – was an officer cadet at Mons.

THE REDOUBT AND ZAYED LINES

Beyond Faraday Hall and the Medical Reception Station, Zayed Lines – named in honour of Sheik Zayed, first President of the United Arab Emirates, which country's generous donation made its building possible – provides living and administrative accommodation for a company of officer cadets. It sits on a site long known as 'the Redoubt' – another hark back to one of several 19th-century practice fortifications.

Further generous overseas gifts are recalled in the names of several sports facilities: the Qaboos Pavilion, the King Hussein Pavilion, the Brunei Stables and the Oman Hall.

FORT NARRIEN

Fort Narrien recalls the service here of another great scientist. Today an area of married quarters for Academy staff, what once stood here was another of the Royal Military College's practice fortifications, named for John Narrien. Narrien, a prominent astronomer of his day, was appointed to the teaching staff in 1814 and served until failing eyesight forced his resignation in 1858. He had an observatory built on top of the mound behind Old College.

BAROSSA

To the north-east of the Academy is an extensive training area where officer cadets receive their earliest instruction in fieldcraft, navigation and tactics. Part wooded and part open heathland, the area has long been known as Barossa Common, after the 1811 Battle of Barossa (southern Spain) in the Peninsular War.